FROM THE EDITOR

For those of us who garden in cold climates, winter is the time for planning and dreaming. And if you are ready to dream big and get some new ideas for your garden, I encourage you to get your cup of hot cocoa, get comfortable, and enjoy this issue of the *Quarterly*.

I'm the kind of rock gardener who is very comfortable with the gardening part but a little bit out of my depth when it comes to the rocks. This is why I am delighted to publish the first article in this issue in which David Pulman and Jeremy Schmidt walk us through every step of placing the stones for a crevice garden on David's new property. I learned a lot getting to watch over their shoulders as this structure came to be.

Next up, I got to pick the brain, by way of an interview, of Ernie DeMarie. If you follow Ernie on social media or know his garden, you'll know that he manages to grow a staggering number of unusual plants – many of them from South Africa – in his New York garden. He shares how he gets these plants to perennialize in his climate, and a fascinating list of South African plants worth trying. I know I'm going to be looking for all of them in this year's SeedEx.

We round out the issue with a little armchair traveling, with Wiert Nieuman taking us on a tour of the Nockberge Biosphere Reserve in the Alps, and Panayoti Kelaidis sharing with us the astonishing beauty and botanical diversity of Patagonia.

If all that armchair traveling is making you itch do to the real thing, then page on to the information about the 2023 Annual General Meeting taking place in Nova Scotia, Canada. It looks stunning.

4

30

18

42

Quarterly

NORTH AMERICAN ROCK GARDEN SOCIETY

VOLUME 81   ISSUE 1

ISSN 1081-0765: USPS no. 0072-960

Is published quarterly in January, April, July and October by the North American Rock Garden Society,

   c/o Bobby Ward, Exec. Sec.
   214 Ashton Hall Lane, Raleigh, NC
   27609-3925

A tax exempt, non-profit organization incorporated under the laws of the State of New Jersey. Periodicals postage is paid in Raleigh, NC, and additional offices.

EDITOR

Joseph Tychonievich
South Bend, Indiana

SUBMISSION DEADLINES

   SPRING ISSUE - February 1
   SUMMER ISSUE - May 1
   FALL ISSUE - August 1
   WINTER ISSUE - November 1

Membership includes a subscription to the *Quarterly* and participation in the seed exchange, as well as other benefits.

Annual Dues: US/Canada regular membership $40, all other countries membership $45. US/Canada Household membership $70. Overseas household membership $75. Patron US/Canda/Overseas $100, Patron household US/Canada/Overseas household $150, Student $15. Institutional membership (defined as herbaria, botanical gardens and institutions of higher learning) $125.

Membership can also be paid online via credit card/Paypall at <www.nargs.org>

ADVERTISING - Contact Joseph Tychonievich at https://www.nargs.org/contact

54

Creating a Crevice Garden: A Shared Journey

DAVID PULMAN and JEREMY SCHMIDT

David

As my wife Clare and I were having COVID-19 catalyzed discussions about whether it made sense for us to leave North Carolina and relocate nearer to family, the subject of the garden was raised. Our Chapel Hill garden, which had undergone a five-year makeover, including the addition of two crevice gardens, was our place, important to us. A place to do satisfying work and a wonderful environment to relax and enjoy ourselves. A decision of family vs. garden didn't take long to make: "we can easily build a new garden" was my assessment (it must have been the wine talking). The decision to move to Georgia was made.

We ended up buying a newly built house, complete with three different types of sod laid over builders' rubble and compacted Georgia clay. A full-on new garden? In the cold light of day, it is not that easy!

However, as we planned the garden, the one constant was that we wanted another crevice garden at the heart of it. The harmony of plant and stone was too much to resist. Our previous two crevice gardens had been built by Jeremy Schmidt, and we had established such a good rapport that I was convinced we could plan a garden from a distance. The design could be an iterative email process and I could get a contractor to do the prep work. Because Jeremy had already taught me how to select and buy stone he could then just drop by for a few days and do his magic. I put the proposal to him and was absolutely delighted when, with great enthusiasm, he accepted the challenge.

Cardboard boxes and turf marking paint help visualize the future location of the crevice garden.

We talked in a relaxed manner about many design topics. The problem I was having was determining the position of the crevice garden relative to other elements of the garden we wanted (herbaceous perennial border, herb garden, woodland garden, Japanese stylistic area). The design tool that helped resolve this was big cardboard boxes and turf marking paint. This visualization process identified the sweet spot in a garden that only had a high to low drop of about four feet (1.2 m).

Jeremy, through a bit of detective work, identified the only bulk source of Permatil (a heat-expanded slate) in the state which, fortuitously, was also a good source of bespoke planting medium. We ended up with 28 cubic yards (21 cubic m) of a Permatil (44%), river sand (28%), worm castings (28%) blend.

Our previous two crevice gardens had allowed us to develop a great way of working. We jointly agree the big design points as Clare and I declare the things we would like to incorporate and Jeremy reflects on the art of the possible. After that I become a rudimentary laborer and coffee maker, and Jeremy does what he does best: stack stone.

Custom planting medium for the new garden.

We agreed on the foundation design. An eighteen-inch-deep (45 cm) cavity that sloped up to twelve inches (30 cm) at the edge would define the work perimeter. A 3000-pound (1360 kg) flat boulder would be positioned to act as a "sitting stone." Clare and I are both fond of the Burren in the west of Ireland so we wanted to incorporate klints (also spelled "clints," blocks of limestone that make up the iconic pavement of the Burren). As much as possible we wanted this to be toddler friendly as our granddaughter would be a frequent visitor. Jeremy suggested six pallets of stone would do the trick.

After a little anxiety, two days before what we called "J-Day," the pre-installation preparation had been completed and Jeremy gave me the good news: his better half, Meghan Fidler, a great stone stacker in her own right, was also coming to Georgia. We were off!

Jeremy

Just a couple of hours after participating online in the February 6, 2021, NARGS Rocks Crevices virtual study day, I received an email from David informing me of his and Clare's decision to relocate. Over the past two decades, the Pulmans created a beautiful stone-based garden, and they had recently commissioned two of my best crevice creations. Suddenly, their exceptional Chapel Hill garden and my part in it was changing hands…

Top: Prepping the site

Bottom: The centerpiece "Sitting Stone" boulder

but that's love in the time of COVID. And in the very next sentence, David invited me to build a crevice feature as a centerpiece in his new garden. Yes…of course, yes! Is there any other reasonable answer to such a proposal? It must have been the beer talking. The decision to travel to Georgia was made.

From Valentine's Day through Halloween, months of emails and phone calls transpired—as if tossing a ball back and forth over a very high wall—all planning our great escarpment. I never felt less than confident about the early November culmination. I had worked with the Pulmans enough to know I would arrive at a worksite approximately like we both imagined, and with lots of great stone. And it was on!

Day Zero

In the waning light of our travel day, David and Clare gave Meghan and me a 360-degree tour of their new home and future garden. During our preamble amble, we were introduced to a wonderfully prepped worksite, complete with a central, optimally pre-set boulder, ready for a crevice garden. That night in the hotel room, I imagined ways to create the most improbable and aesthetically appealing natural design in the space and timeframe provided. I fast-forwarded through millennia; I witnessed natural forces pushing, bending, folding, and weathering the crevice formation up to present day, and then watched the plantings mature for the next five years. I built and bulldozed the Pulman's crevice garden several times that night in my mind. Meghan says I dig in my sleep. It's probably true.

Day One

Six pallets of stone were staged conveniently adjacent to the worksite. David sent me several pictures of crevice and klint stone options from a large Atlanta area supply yard. We settled on three stone shapes, all branded as part of the Tennessee Fieldstone series, and all apparently from the same quarry. Three pallets of Capstone provided the main body of the crevices. These stones ranged somewhere between stout quadrilaterals and isosceles triangles, averaging 30-200 lbs (13 to 90 kg) each, and five to eight inches (13-20 cm) thick. Two pallets of Long Stack were flagged for use as steppable, plantable, klint stones. These were consistently French-fry-shaped, and five to twelve inches (13-30cm) thick depending on orientation. Finally, one pallet of Medium Veneer was selected primarily to define the edges in conjunction with the large stones. These were three to six inches (7.6-15 cm) thick and 10 to 50 lbs (4.5- 23 kg), really just a smaller version of the Capstones. Three shapes and sizes of stone, all from the same quarry, and possessing handsomely weathered-but-squared faces and edges. We could not have custom ordered more optimal crevice stones. All that just to describe our rocks?! Yes. Day one, we cut the cages—thus activating the stone.

Accompanying the placement of the first stones was an hour of ritualistic pacing, pondering, and face-scrunching. I've learned from experience that 25% or more of the total crevice installation will share similar spacing/ orientation/dialect with the initial five-or-so contiguous stones. So, when we stacked the first stones, we had already mentally committed to the macro-concepts of the installation.

Site prepped with the central boulder in place.

The first of the flat klint-inspired pavement in place.

For this project, the klint was the obvious starting point. We took our time determining how the klint would interface and aesthetically elevate the large, central boulder—and then how the klint would transition into raised crevices. By the time we stacked the first five klint stones, we had committed to the grain, spacing, and location of one-third of the total square footage of the project. By the end of the first day we had set about 50 stones, all as part of the klint.

Day Two

For two reasons, we ignored the klint at the start of day two. We focused our efforts instead as far away from our first day's work as possible—stacking raised crevices at the downhill extent of the installation. Reason one: after spending an entire day to move through only about 50 stones, our calculated pivot bypassed the "stackers block" we encountered the previous afternoon. Shifting our location within the crevice garden footprint provided an instant plethora of easy stacking choices; and suddenly the project was moving as fast as we could place stone. Reason two: by stacking from low to high, each consecutive stone was ready to support the next stone—a valuable lesson I've had to learn more than once.

After we bent and folded several stones into place, Meghan discovered an opportunity a few feet away to incorporate a small rubble island of misfit rocks. Separated from the main crevices by the walkable expanse constructed during day one, the small feature added a measure of balance to the large central boulder, and gave a voice to stone less likely to fit elsewhere in the project. She even re-homed a few "impossible-to-stack" quartz rocks native to the property. I've had excellent success with similar small rubble accents in previous crevice installations, including at the Pulmans' former garden. When done right, a patch, a vein, or a pocket of rubble is no less aesthetic or plantable. And Meghan stacked it right. Joined together, "unusable" stones serve to heighten the story being told, all while stretching stone supply.

Another 80 puzzle pieces registered, and a bigger picture began taking shape. Like long brushstrokes, stones reached out to make first contact with the central boulder. And, out of nowhere, rocks conjured stairs and a bisecting path. Edges were becoming defined. The space was evolving into place.

Working on getting the stones in place.

Day Three

To avoid blowing through all the ideal, easy-to-place stones before completion, I stacked through the stone supply as linearly as possible. To accommodate this tactical randomization, I non-selectively siphoned a few stones from each pallet into a small, 10-15 stone, queue available within arms' reach of where I was working. The recurrent short-term objective was to empty the queue before staging the next stone amalgamation. Adhering to this discipline while freely skipping around to multiple stacking points guarantees consistent material supply throughout the duration of crevice garden installation. I've found that this practice not only supports a healthy supply chain, but also facilitates an unlikely alliance between capricious creativity and laser-focused objectivity. More specifically, if stone choices for the stacking challenge at hand are restricted only to what is within reach, then the meticulous comprehension of each stone's shape and attitude is also within reach. A boundless imagination can apply this detailed short-term memory queue to execute perfect stone combinations. Whereas, to select the "perfect" stone from the pallet is rather short-sighted in comparison.

The stones beginning to become a unified garden.

Flat stones serve as a walkway through the garden

Why such a protracted and roundabout introduction to day three? Because we were halfway through our stone supply and halfway through the project. If we had been cherry-picking in the first two days, we would already have run out of cherries. With the exception of making short work of the Long Stack stones to finish the klint, and setting aside a few large stepping stones, we were systematically slicing through stone pallets like one would slice through of loaf of bread.

Also, Day Three
Mentally and physically—and more so emotionally—day three was unavoidably a difficult haul. Physical exhaustion can be mitigated by redistributing the load across a network of 600 muscles, but there is only one brain to conduct their orchestral movements. Somewhere beyond the halfway point of every multi-day crevice construction project I've completed, whether over a span of four days or over two years, momentum stalls, and a doldrum settles in. Mental vision blurs as completion remains elusively out of sight. Every inch of progress requires willpower, muscle memory, discipline, and an exaggerated deep breath between the placement of each stone.

View showing the flat klint area radiating out from the central boulder

Stacking challenges intensified during the second half of the Pulmans' crevice project. We were faced with compounding constraints like uniting disjunct stacking points into a contiguous crevice garden. No more skipping around from point to point. We had to close out sections we avoided earlier. Regardless of how delightful the Tennessee Fieldstone was to have and to hold at the beginning of the project, some muscles were as worn out as my Pearl Jam playlist on Pandora. It became more difficult to stay receptive to the unique details and personality each rock had to offer to the story we were stacking. By lunch the third day, we weren't running low on great stones, we were running short on mental bandwidth. The sun advanced as it does across the southern November sky, while Meghan and I pressed on to the best of our ability. We moved one stone at a time; we spoke to each other one word at a time. Day three was really just one quarter of the project timeline, but it felt much longer. Yet each piece was placed with great care and consideration—there was no compromise. Another stone set…a pause for Clare's ham and cheese sandwiches on multi-grain bread, sliced diagonally, with crust removed…a diet soda…a deep breath…pick up another stone from the queue…a granola bar…a sip of David's scalding hot afternoon coffee... and then a deep breath. Another stone set. By the time the shadows stretched across the crevices late that afternoon, the end was in sight.

Day four

What could possibly be more important than the first 95% of the project? Answer: the final 5%. After all, if the last few stones are noticeably thrown together in frustration or surrender or haste, the entire crevice garden will be defined by that small percentage of futility. If the final decisions are enacted with similar confidence and passion as when the first stones were liberated from their cages, then a unified story is told. If no one can point out the last few stones in the project, I take it as a good sign.

With the completed project close at hand, we hit day four with renewed energy, our brains were synchronized and sharp. We were as hungry to close out the final voids as we were to stock our opening statements on a clean slate. There was a granddaughter ramp to engineer behind the central boulder for high-speed toddler access, but the main challenge of the day was to shovel 1.5 cubic yards (1.1 cubic m) of surplus crevice soil out of the way of the final edge and crevices. David helped us greatly with hauling the soil mix further to the side, closing out the klint, and with laying several steppers for the ramp. We also worked with David and Clare to select, move, and place a toro (Japanese stone lantern) at the apex of the crevice garden. They

Stone toro (Japanese lantern) in place on the stonework'

had transported three such stone lanterns from their previous North Carolina garden, so we had three to choose from on site. Clare was right—the first toro we chose was too large for the space. We took a breather, regrouped, and moved a slightly smaller toro into place. The day was delightfully punctuated by a visit from premier horticulturists Lisa Bartlett and Ozzie Johnson—the Pulmans new crevice garden was already drawing people together! Lisa and Ozzie dropped off a beautiful Japanese native *Allium kiiense* as a crevice warming gift. By noon on day four, we finished the project, opening the next chapter in the story of these stones.

David and Clare's investment in the planning and preparation, and our ongoing communication ensured that we were on the same page from the start. In the context of love for family, and a passion for nature, David and Clare provided very clear expectations of how they intended to inhabit the central rocky feature; and immersed in an environment of non-stop hospitality, we were supplied with exactly what we needed to accomplish the Pulmans' goals. Truly, Meghan and I are honored to be a part of this garden. These stones were drawn together to tell the story of family—from the ground up.

Construction of the crevice garden complete and ready for planting.

David's last word

With the physical crevice garden complete (everyone who visits is mightily impressed) it is time to turn attention to the planting— in my mind something equally difficult! I have brought my list of plants that did well in North Carolina, which is a good place to start. There will be a trawl of the market place but any suggestions from NARGS members will gratefully be received!

Time is not infinite as there are the other elements of the garden to be installed and then planted up. This will be a more stressful process as in addition to "doing a garden" I have to build relationships with the contractors from scratch. I anticipate a more hands-on process and if you wish to follow progress then check out the blog at AndAllenGarden.com.

No matter how it all turns out, this is a lot of fun!

The new garden ten weeks after planting.

A CONVERSATION WITH ERNIE DEMARIE

interviewed by JOSEPH TYCHONIEVICH

What is your background in horticulture?

I have been into growing plants since I remember. I am told I followed my great-grandmother in Bluefield, West Virginia (where I was born) around her garden putting sticks in the ground when I was four years old. I remember having a small garden at a house where we rented in Yonkers, New York, when we moved there when I was five years old. So I have always gardened, but generally on a small scale while I was young since I didn't have much land nor parents that encouraged gardening. I then went to Cornell University where I earned a bachelor's degree in Horticulture (it was called Floriculture and Ornamental Horticulture back then) and when I came out of college I realized that there wasn't much I could do with just a bachelor's degree other than perhaps work in a nursery, which is not my thing. So I went back to college (again Cornell) and earned a master's degree in Agricultural and Occupational Education and teaching certifications in biology and general science. I then ran a horticulture program at Prospect Heights High School in Brooklyn, New York, in the early 1980s.

In 1983, I took a trip to Botswana and South Africa and was completely amazed by the Cape flora. I thought to myself that I should be studying this and so I returned to Cornell to earn a PhD in horticulture. I had the intention, as did most of the graduate students in the department at the time, of becoming a professor. The harsh reality was that, by late 1990 when I finished, professorships were hard to find due to hiring adjuncts and postdocs. I ended up working at New York Botanical Garden (NYBG) as curator of the desert plant collection for six years. I liked what I did but did not like the salary, the internal politics, and the lack of job security. I learned a lot by growing a vast array of plants, and that was fun. I had a small garden at home.

I decided to return to high school teaching as I wanted job security, better pay, and a pension. So I ended up teaching biology, AP (Advanced Placement) Biology, AP Environmental Science, and other courses at Christopher Columbus High School in the Bronx, New York. While there, I would sometimes swing by NYBG on a Friday after school and help out a bit with my former plant collection and talk plants.

I then decided to apply to schools in the suburbs and got a job at Horace Greeley in Chappaqua, New York. Once there, I began to prepare a garden of a decent size right outside the door where I usually enter the school. Together with my AP students, we enlarged the garden over the first few years I was there and I grew many species and cultivars there. At one point, I made a list and there were something like over 300 different kinds of plants in the gardens. In late 2012, I moved with my wife to a larger house on 0.64 acres (0.26 hec) and began to turn the entire property into gardens. This process took three or four years to accomplish, and even now I redo some areas or change it up a bit. It is here on our property in Briarcliff Manor, New York, that I have been able to finally realize my gardening dreams. Well, most of them. I would really love to have a greenhouse one day, but with LED lights and shelves I am able to grow many indoor plants in winter especially. Our property also features large patios where potted plants can go out for the summer.

Can you describe the climate and conditions in your garden?

We are on the edge of USDA Zone 7 at this point, bordering on Zone 6. The lowest temperature I have seen was -1°F (-18°C) one night. Normally, we get a winter low of maybe three to nine degrees Fahrenheit (-16 to -12°C). Summer high temperatures usually are in the 80s (26-32°C) but can go into the 90s (32-37°C) or the 70s (21-26°C), which is the best for most of what I grow. Hot wet spells are the worst as they can cause rot on plants like delospermas. Our nights are cooler than the days and hot nights are relatively rare. Older gardeners in the area tell me that it used to be colder. The climate is temperate, with last frost usually in early to mid April, and first frost around November 10th, but it can come in late October some years.

What kinds of plants do you like to grow?

The gardens are mostly sunny, with few shrubs other than roses, and no large trees. I grow mostly herbaceous perennials, self-sowing annuals, and bulbs. There are some special areas and gardens. For example, there is a large garden dedicated to South African plants, though these plants can also be found in just about all of my gardens.

There is a small section near the house and another spot where I grow plants I collected in China or grew from collected seeds. I have several roses, both species and older types, and a few tea roses, too. Most of my peonies are grown from seed; they are mainly hybrids with a few species. There are enough kniphofia species here that there is always one or more in bloom. I grow a lot of *Crinum bulbispermum* as well, which are beginning to self-sow, something I thought they weren't supposed to be able to do in our cold-winter climate.

There are a lot of unusual plants here, including a number that I have collected elsewhere, usually as seed. I also grow a lot from the seed exchanges and seed companies in South Africa, the United Kingdom, and elsewhere.

Crinum bulbispermum in full bloom

Indoors, I grow a sizable collection of winter-growing South African oxalis, pelargoniums, and geophytes. They reside under lights in the two-car garage while the cars sit outside for winter. One has to have priorities after all.

I know you for your incredible collection of plants from South Africa. How did you get interested in this group?

I became interested in South African plants when I did a summer of community gardening based from the Brooklyn Botanic Garden (BBG). There I met Betty Scholtz, who once was president of the BBG. She was from South Africa and introduced me to *Veld and Flora*, the magazine of the Botanical Society of South Africa. The society gave members abroad a free seed allotment at the time, which was a great incentive to join. I took

Pelargonium luridum

my first trip to South Africa in August of 1984 and I was just stunned by the diversity of the Cape flora. Betty also set me up with some contacts in South Africa who helped me better understand the flora.

I grew a large collection of pelargonium species in the greenhouse at Cornell. I brought much of that collection with me to NYBG, where a decent portion remains to this day. While at NYBG, I experimented with growing South African flora outside near the greenhouse and in a special bed I prepared in a nearby area. I wrote about that garden for *Veld and Flora* some years ago. I grew South African flora in my small gardens at my parent's house and also in the school gardens along with other plants. Though I do not upkeep the school gardens like I used to due to the demands of the home gardens and a full-time teaching job, there are still such things as *Amaryllis belladonna* and *Pelargonium luridum* that come up every year by the wall of the building that creates a warmer microclimate for them.

Here in the home gardens, I will protect some of the South African and other zone-pushing plants with wood chips that I put on them in December or, at the latest, early January. This allows me to grow things like gerberas as perennials here. In spring, I move the mulch aside and use it in paths or just let it rot to improve the soil.

Can you recommend some off-the-beaten-track South African plants you think NARGS members should try growing?

Helichrysum splendidum is a vigorous plant with silvery fragrant foliage that repels plant-eating mammalian vermin. In hard winters here it will often die back to near the base but regrows fast. It has few flowers after hard winters, but in milder winters there is little to no dieback and it can get huge and have lots of small yellow strawflowers in yarrow-like clusters in June.

Haplocarpha scaposa has rosettes of attractive foliage from which emerge long stems with big bright yellow daisies, sort of like a gerbera but with better foliage. It also blooms off and on all growing season and would be reliable in Zone 7 and probably into Zone 6 with a little winter protection.

Left: *Helichrysum splendidum* Right: *Haplocarpha scaposa*

Delosperma congestum

Gerbera jamesonii, the ancestor of the cultivated gerbera, is a beautiful red daisy that looks nicer and more wildflower-like than the commonly cultivated sorts. It mass blooms in June and a few flowers appear sporadically afterward. A thick winter mulch of wood chips, maybe six inches (15 cm) or so deep, has kept it solidly perennial here for several years.

Kniphofia caulescens is the toughest and hardiest of the genus. The flowers vary from red to yellow, most often coming in a bicolored form. It blooms once in June and will self-sow here. No winter here has killed it so far, though for optimal appearance I cut the off old, tattered, winter-damaged foliage in the spring.

Kniphofia northiae has some of the least attractive flowers of the genus and is not a generous bloomer, but its foliage totally rocks. It looks like a giant, wide-leaved tillandsia.

Crinum bulbispermum is a must-have. It is slow from seed and isn't a fast offsetter, but it is very hardy and requires no protection here. It produces lots of blooms in June and sporadic ones afterward. I have so much of it here that there is almost always one in flower somewhere in the garden, even after the main bloom season. The foliage is nice too. All it lacks is the sweet fragrance of its more tender relatives.

Delospermas come in many forms, but I'd suggest *Delospema congestum* (it goes by other names, too) as the hardiest. It has yellow flowers with white centers in early spring. Some of the magenta/hot pink sorts (e.g., *D. ashtonii and D. cooperii*) can flower for a very long time and are vigorous growers in sunny well-drained areas.

Top left: *Gerbera jamesonii*   Top right: *Kniphofia caulescens*
Bottom left: *Kniphofia northiae*   Bottom right: *Crinum bulbispermum*

*Galtonia candicans (*Syn. *Ornithogalum candicans)* is easy to find and is reliably hardy here. It makes nice spires of white flowers and the seed is easy to germinate to grow more.

Agapanthus 'Old Wayside Clone' is a form that Ellen Hornig sold from her former Seneca Hills nursery. It is a dwarf blue one and may be a form of *A. campanulatus.* It is hardy here without protection and would be the best choice in the genus for a rock garden.

Some forms of *Gladiolus papilio* have nice markings in the flowers and are very hardy. They can form a thick stand rather fast. In nature, it grows in wet areas but will grow fine in regular garden soil.

Phygelius is a reliable genus here, it is composed of two species that are hard to distinguish and which very well could be one in my opinion. Several cultivars exist in reds, yellows, pinkish, and salmon colors. Even when they die back to the ground they are quick to sprout again and flower. They can form spreading colonies rather fast in areas they like.

Agapanthus 'Old Wayside Clone'

Top left: *Gladiolus papilio* Top right: *Phygelius* sp.

Bottom: *Galtonia candicans*

Top left: *Artemisia afra*   Top right: *Gazania linearis*
Bottom: *Diascia integerrima*

Artemesia afra has pleasing foliage, both aromatically and visually. It is hardy here and even reseeds a bit. It can benefit from a partial cutback in spring to keep it from getting too tall.

Gazanias are lovely things but so far only *Gazania linearis* is hardy, and more so some years than others. Seeds and plants are readily available here, and it will bloom well if treated as an annual. Flowers are yellow, some having nice black central rings or spots at the petal base.

Diascia integerrima is a nice, hardy diascia for a rock garden. There is a cultivar in the US, 'Coral Canyon', that I have killed a couple of times but seed I got from Silverhill Seeds produced plants that have thrived for several years.

Wahlenbergia undulata is the South African answer to campanula. It has spreading roots that produce masses of blue upturned flowers all summer long. It grows easily from seed or division and is hardy here. It can vary a bit in different localities in South Africa from what appear to be more robust to more gracile forms.

Know a rock gardener you'd like to see interviewed in the Quarterly? *Let me know via the Contact Us page on NARGS.org*

Wahlenbergia undulata

ALPINE FLOWERS IN THE NOCKBERGE BIOSPHERE RESERVE

WIERT NIEUMAN

For a plant lover, a walk in a nature reserve is, first of all, a search for unusual plants. The Nockberge Mountains in the state of Carinthia in Austria are an ideal destination for that.

In 1976, UNESCO launched the concept of a biosphere reserve with the aim of preserving large areas of cultural and natural landscapes throughout the world. The state of Carinthia wanted to create a skiing paradise in the Nockberge that would attract tourists and bring in a lot of money, but it had not taken into account the locals. Through a referendum, in which 94% of the residents voted against this plan, the ski paradise was rejected. They did not want large-scale tourism that would affect the area, but rather ecotourism, although that word did not exist at the time.

The Nockalmstrasse, a scenic road through the area, was already built when the ski park plan was dropped and on January 1, 1987, and a large part of the region was named a national park. In 2012, it received the coveted status of Biosphärenpark (Biosphere park). Now it is an area for hikers and nature lovers instead of winter sports enthusiasts.

Opposite: *Dryas octopetala* in the Nockberge Mountains

The Nockberge Mountains

The Nockberge are not comparable to other mountains in the Alps. They are more like giant hills than mountains. The peaks are rounded and mostly grass-covered, and although the highest peaks are over 2400 meters (7875 ft) high, they still retain a hill-like appearance. Most of these mountains are acidic, but there is also a strip of limestone and dolomitic rock running north to south for up to three kilometers (1.9 miles). The rain that falls on this porous part sinks down and comes back to the surface at Bad Kleinkirchheim, the main village in this region. By then, the water has warmed up to 36°C (97°F). Bad Kleinkirchheim has been a spa town since the 17th century, but agriculture was the main source of income for the population until well into the 20th century. Only in the last few decades have people been living off tourism, because, although the intended ski paradise in the Nockberge never materialized, there are ski slopes around the village with a total length of 103 kilometers (64 miles) and it is also a popular vacation area in the summer months.

The Nockalmstrasse is a 35-kilometer (22-mile) toll road through the Nockberge. This road runs from Ebene Reichenau in the southeast to Innerkrems on the northwest side of the mountains. In 1981, this road, with a total of 52 hairpin bends, opened to traffic. It is truly a tourist route with many rest and parking areas and magnificent panoramas. Plan at least one day to drive this route and expect to make stops very often. From May to July, it is like a big flower festival, and you can often photograph beautiful flowers from the car, though it is much better to park somewhere and take long walks.

A very nice place is the area around the Wildebensee. This is an idyllic lake you can walk around in half an hour. You can see that cattle also come here regularly because in some places there is a lot of sorrel, *Rumex alpinus*, a sign that the soil here is enriched with manure. The ever-fascinating *Veratrum album* grows here and *Rhododendron ferrugineum* indicates that the rock and soil are acidic.

Windebensee Lake

Top: *Saponaria pumila*   Bottom: *Dianthus sylvestris*

A typical representative of the eastern Alps is *Saponaria pumila*. It is
a low soapwort species that is completely hidden under blooms during
the flowering period and in the Nockberge it is very prominent. What a
pleasure to look at all those different tufts of soapwort! Sometimes they
are in narrow crevices in the rock, and sometimes just among the grass.
With difficulty, we pull away from this gem and our gaze is drawn to a real
carnation. The species we see here is *Dianthus sylvestris* subsp. *sylvestris*.
It is a carnation with large pink flowers that usually grows in stony places
along roadsides and in rubble slopes. It does not grow very tall and the
stems are somewhat floppy so they often droop under the weight of flowers
and buds.

The sky blue of *Myosotis alpestris* or alpine forget-me-not is also not to be missed. It is unbelievable how blue it can be. Oh well, it's just a forget-me-not, you don't stop for that, do you? But sit down, take a closer look at the flowers and you'll discover that some of them have a nice yellow throat and others have a white one. Once the flower has been pollinated, the yellow edge around the opening fades and that's a sign to pollinators that there's nothing left to get. You can walk from blue to blue because you also come across rampions in the Nockberge. You will find *Phyteuma orbiculare*, which grows up to 50 cm (20 in) high, and the only 15 cm (6 inch) high *Phyteuma hemisphaericum* both coloring the meadows with their blue flowers.

Left: *Myosotis alpestris*   Right: *Phyteuma orbiculare*

Top: *Valeriana celtica* subsp. *norica*

Bottom: *Geum montanum*

Along the paths, the alpine rock-clover, *Lotus alpinus*, grows everywhere. Because of the altitude, the poor growing areas, and the light, the flowers are much more intense in color than those of the common rock-clover we find in the lowlands. The flowers of *Geum montanum* are also yellow and, after flowering, the seed pods form a wild and photogenic capsule. In acidic and somewhat more humid places grows *Tofieldia calyculata*, an inconspicuous little plant that we encounter very often in the Alps. It is said to be an indicator for lime, though in reality can grow on all types of soil, provided it is not too dry. The capriciousness of the rocks and soil types in terms of acidity is evident when we suddenly see a stone that appears to be covered with *Sempervivum montanum* subsp. *stiriacum*, a house garlic species with striking red flowers that is bound to acidic soils.

A phenomenon of the Nockberge is *Valeriana celtica* subsp. *norica*, known there as speik or norischer speik. It is a small, inconspicuous plant that grows there in large numbers and whose spicy fragrance is everywhere in the summer months. The roots of this plant contain valerian oil and because of this medicinal and soothing oil, the plant was dug up en masse and exported. The lime-free alpine meadows between 1800 and 2000 m (5900-6500 feet) where this species can be found have even been given a special name, the Speikböden. In earlier times, the landlord had the exclusive right to have this speik harvested. Today, people who have a permit and can harvest the roots from mid-August until September 8th. The harvestable roots are taken away and the rest are carefully planted again. Only after four years can they be harvested again. Speik, sometimes also called speick, is still a popular product because it cannot yet be synthesized, and the soap and other products made from it fetch a good price. From mid-June onwards, flowering plants can be seen everywhere, but because the plant only grows to 15 cm (6 inches) in height and the flowers are small and inconspicuous, you have to look for them. Have you been to the Nockberge as a plant lover and not seen a speik? That is an unforgivable blunder! Everyone in the region knows the plant and in Bad Kleinkirchheim there is even a sculpture of it, four meters (13 feet) high.

From Bad Kleinkirchheim you can take the Kaiserburgbahn to over 2,000 m (6560 feet) and there, from the end of May to the middle of July, are hundreds of plant photo models. A stone's throw from the cable car the ground is speckled with one of the most beautiful bellflowers, *Campanula alpina*. This species is found only in the eastern Alps. This bellflower has a leaf rosette and above it a single stem on which sit the relatively large bell-shaped, pendulous flowers. The flowers are larger than those of the ubiquitous *Campanula barbata*, and the plant is taller and has more flowers than *Campanula alpestris* which grows on limestone in the southwestern Alps. This gem can be grown as a rock garden plant but you will not be able to enjoy it for very many years because it is not long-lived in the garden. Because this is an acidic area, you can also see *Soldanella pusilla*. It is a small one, but oh so beautiful! It is in full bloom at the edge of snow fields. Lie down next to the flowers on the ground and enjoy all those beautiful bells.

Campanula alpina

Loiseleuria procumbens

Even smaller is *Loiseleuria procumbens* (Syn. *Kalmia procumbens*). In places where the wind blows everything away even in winter this relative of the rhododendron still manages to hold its own. In June, this groundcover plant blooms with pink flowers which are followed by red seed pods. *Dryas octopetala*, or eighth star, can be seen everywhere, especially on limestone, but also on acidic soil. They are always photogenic when perched on a boulder and the white flowers stand out beautifully against the blue sky.

On the other side of the village, you can take the Brunnachbahn to 1900 m (6200 feet) in the Biosphärenpark and go for beautiful walks. The white-flowering *Minuartia rupestris* and *Silene pusilla* are common, but not conspicuous. They are completely outshown by the pasqueflower, *Pulsatilla alpina* subsp. *austroalpina* with white flowers on slender stems above a bed of finely divided leaves. They are truly everywhere and each group is more photogenic than the next. Near the hamlet of Valkert are large groups of rose root, *Rhodiola rosea*, known for its medicinal properties.

Steep mountain paths and deep ravines are a rarity in the Nockberge; however, a wide selection of flowering plants in large numbers is almost guaranteed in the period from late May to mid-July. With cable cars from Bad Kleinkirchheim you can quickly get to 2000 m (65000 feet) and once at the top, the hiking pace is at most one or two km per hour because the many plant species constantly force you to your knees. On these hikes, the plants are the goal and the distance covered is of secondary importance.

Silene pusilla

Top: *Pulsatilla alpina subsp. austroalpina*

Bottom: *Rhodiola rosea*

PLEASURES OF PATAGONIA

PANAYOTI KELAIDIS

photos by

GLENN GUETENBERG and PATRICE VAN FLEET

Patagonia evokes the sense of the remote to most of us in the Northern Hemisphere—the seeming ends of the earth. In this strange era of COVID-19, Argentina turned out to be a fantastic destination for a number of reasons which will hopefully be manifest in the course of my writing.

As this issue of the *Quarterly* goes to print, twenty of our fellow members will be tracing the very steps I'll be describing in this article. They were supposed to go on this trip in 2021, however, Argentina had sealed its borders so that even Argentines such as Marcela Ferreyra were stranded abroad for long periods. But not long after the trip had been canceled, those restrictions were lifted. Members were polled if they were willing to still go and a few did rally, and we did a "dry run" of this year's trip. Last year followed a number of the driest years in Patagonian history: ski areas canceled their seasons for lack of snow, and little rain fell. We on the trip would have never guessed this: we found a wealth of plants, although we did get a little weary of the locals telling us "how much better it ought to be". I can only imagine what this year's tour is finding after a very snowy winter!

A special note of thanks must be given to Marcela Ferreyra, a retired professor of botany who has written a number of books on the Argentine flora, mostly concentrating on Patagonia, who was our tour guide for this trip. She is well known to many NARGS members, having spoken at several North American meetings, and given talks to many chapters. Her depth of learning is matched by her wonderful tour guide skills. A trip with Marcela is a trip of a lifetime.

The province of Neuquen, which we traversed from south to north, weaving into and out of various valleys to the Andes, has to be one of the most scenically enchanting spots on the planet. The Andes here consist of dozens of volcanoes, some still smoldering ominously, many clad with glaciers, and jutting as far as the eye can see. On their lower slopes in this province, they are clad for the most part with a forest consisting primarily of monkey puzzle trees (*Araucaria araucana*) referred to here as "pinos" yet are utterly dissimilar in feel from their distant North American pine cousins.

Top: *Araucaria araucana*
Bottom: Gaucho herding sheep

Maihuenia poeppigii

Their bark reminds me of what the skin of some dinosaur must have looked like, and their broad needles and branching also evoke Jurassic sensations. You half expect a Velociraptor to leap out from behind one of them!

And of course, there is the rolling, sometimes grassy, sometimes rocky, Patagonian steppe stretching eastward from the base of the Andes: here we often passed herds of sheep, cattle, or horses driven by gauchos towards the summer pastures. I'm not sure it would be much different in other years, but one of the most haunting charms for me of this entire trip was the utter lack of kitschy touristic signage, the clutter of commercialism that has sullied most gorgeous touristic venues in Europe and North America. Mind you, there are superb amenities in all the scenic lakeside towns, many boasting state-of-the-art ski areas. What they were missing were tourists and the noisy marketing they seem to attract.

We arrived in Bariloche on a crystal clear day, the long, serrated outline of the Andes stretching for hundreds of miles north and south reflected in the navy blue waters of 23-mile (37 km) long Nahel Huapi Lake. The entire region is encompassed by an enormous national park. The west end of the lake is bordered by lush, maritime forests of giant *Nothofagus* festooned with *Usnea* lichen where we explored the first day and found a variety of calceolarias, showy orchids, and many other wildflowers in full bloom. The east end of this same lake is surrounded by the beginning of the Patagonian steppe where we found our first rosulate violets and gorgeous cacti including *Maihuenia patagonica* with rose petals which, alas, were closed.

Top: *Oreopolus glacialis*   Bottom: *Mulinum spinosum*

Patagonian steppe is renowned for the enormous number of cushion plants that occur here, quite a few of which (like *Oreopolus glacialis*) are also found above treeline on the Andes nearby. *Oreopolus* is in the Rubiaceae, forming dense mounds like its distant Eurasian cousins in *Asperula*—but the bright yellow color and subshrubby habit are quite different. It formed loose mats here and there along our journey in the steppe but saved its big show for the high peaks. The most widespread and abundant plant on the steppe seemed to be *Mulinum spinosum*, which some botanists have now transferred to *Azorella*, which are generally much more compact in growth. *Mulinum* forms taller, more airy, welcoming cushions studded with yellow bloom—but don't be fooled! It's quite prickly.

I remember being surprised looking back at San Carlos from a vantage point on the steppe to see masses of yellow evening primoses (*Oenothera odorata*). Everything seemed so exotic up to that point, but this evening primrose recalls a half dozen species that grow commonly across the United States. We were to encounter these strangely familiar links again and again. Our two continents have obviously shared floristic elements over the eons.

Oenothera odorata

Left: *Ourisia fragrans*   Right: *Austrocactus coxii*

On our third day, we had acclimatized enough to take a cable car to the summit of Cathedral Hill (Cerro Catedral), the principal ski area near Bariloche, and a floristically rich destination if there ever was one. Few spectacles are more stirring than hiking on a brilliant spring day on top of a mountain with panoramic views of much of Patagonia. Here is where we saw the bright yellow *Oreopolus* staining whole hillsides yellow and our first alpine rosulate violas. *Viola petraea* and *V. sacculus* were both quite common here, but not seen again on the trip. Another alpine I was delighted to encounter was *Ourisia fragrans*, growing in cool crevices where you would find primulas in the northern hemisphere, and it does resemble a primula more than a penstemon or veronica to which it is more closely related. We found this several times at lofty alpine sites and I kept forgetting to sniff it and see if it is indeed "fragrans."

Bariloche is the northwesternmost town in Río Negro province. Heading northward from there, we quickly entered and spent the next twelve days in Neuquen province, the main focus of our trip. Here we proceeded on highways skirting the foothills of the Andes, weaving into and out of the major river drainages leading to the Atlantic to the east. We would stop from time to time on the steppe when Marcela would spy some special plant. We would tumble out and find far more than we'd expected. Along the road paralleling the Alumine river, someone noticed the glint of a cactus flower: it turned out to be *Austrocactus coxii* forming formidable mounds like some giant Southwestern hedgehog cactus. Luckily, they were in peak of bloom for us, a strange blend of orange and yellow—almost bronze. This is a tint you never find in north temperate columnar cacti. One clump was so spectacular that every one of us took many pictures of it from various angles.

As we followed a river up towards the Cordillera, the first "pinos" came to view—often especially rugged araucarias whipped into picturesque bonsai forms by the lowland winds. The forests thickened, and a crystal blue lake appeared with a few hotels tactfully tucked here and there and some quaint villages adding a human touch to the scene. I realized at one point that the great Swiss lakes might have been like this centuries ago. This is what Tahoe must have been like in the 19th Century. Let's hope that Argentina can avoid having its fantastic lake country overdeveloped.

Each of these lakeside resorts had access to alpine heights nearby, and we had many vigorous hikes at trailheads near each one. Again and again, we would find a variety of alpines—cushions, shrubby sorts, and the inevitable azorellas and rosulate violas. We found *Calandrinia colchaguensis* growing especially lushly in moist swales above the treeline near Copahue, looking so similar to *Lewisia* in its form (they are, of course, related). The flowers varied from pale pink to deep rose. *Calandrinia affinis* was likewise quite often encountered, although the biggest colonies we found were on the steppe, another example of the shared flora of these two very different ecosystems separated by thousands of meters elevation.

Another plant we found at most of our stops was *Rhodolirium andicola*, a truly

Calandrinia colchaguensis

gorgeous amaryllid with bright rose-red flowers. These grew in large drifts on many alpine meadows, but also sparingly on the steppe.

Returning to the steppe from Copahue, we found what became a highlight of the trip for me: I know the scarlet gorse (*Anarthrophyllum desideratum*) only grows farther to the South. I was not aware that that species had a dazzling orange-yellow cousin (*Anarthrophyllum burkartii*). We only found this "tangerine gorse" once, on a flat stretch of steppe looking much like any other only here it was studded with enormous cushions bristling with bicolored yellow-orange pea flowers. All of us go through life with a list of plants we yearn to see in nature and perhaps one day grow. There is another list of those spectacular plants we don't know, and finding them is even more delightful. Tangerine gorse leapt to the top of that list.

Above: *Rhodolirium andicola*
Opposite: *Anarthrophyllum burkartii* studding the steppe with orange blossoms

Viola trochlearis

One stretch of the steppe was especially full of treasures near Laguna Blanca. Here is where we found *Viola trochlearis*, an outlandish rosulate violet with foliage stitched as in fine brown lace, with coy flowers poking out here and there. On a similar unpromising stretch of steppe below Laguna Epulafquen, we found dozens of extraordinary rosettes of *Viola rubromarginata* on the dusty gravel between tufts of grass. Here the amazing rosettes are fringed with fine hair, with a distinct colored margin around the edges—and the flowers are wonderfully speckled white and purple. I am sure dozens, possibly hundreds of photos were snapped here by our group!

We had debated coming up to this lake, our last outing of the trip. The view of the massive Andes rising at the west end of the lake was one of the most imposing of the trip. And not far from the east end of the lake we found the bright, burnished-bronze flowered *Austrocactus hibernus*—utterly distinct in form and flower from all we'd seen up to now. Here the cactus made compact mounds of procumbent stems. We all sprawled trying to catch the snow-dotted Andes behind the plant. So strange that this genus we were to find again and again is so rarely grown in cactus collections or gardens.

These are but a few of the highlights of a trip I would love nothing more than to retrace all over again! And Marcela and her travel agency are making this tour available next year to NARGS. My advice is to hop on it! I can easily imagine this becoming a perennial event for our society. I can't think of anywhere that offers such spectacular scenery, rich flora and exotic ambiance—all in a country that is friendly, secure, and welcoming.

Top: *Viola rubromarginata*   Bottom: *Austrocactus hibernus*

NARGS 2023

Rocks, Plants, Habitats

June 8-11 Nova Scotia

NARGS23.org

You are invited to come to Nova Scotia, Canada, to see our coastal barrens, orchids, woodland plants, and rock gardens. The conference takes place from June 8-11 at the Dalhousie University Agricultural Campus in Truro, Nova Scotia, the site of the recently expanded Limestone Alpine addition to Bicentennial Rock Garden.

The conference will start on Thursday afternoon June 8, with a tour of the Rock Garden and Limestone Alpine Garden featured in the Fall, 2022, NARGS *Quarterly* (see https://www.nargs.org/article/evolution-rock-garden). These gardens were created by Bernard Jackson in 2002 and 2018 and maintained by Friends of the Garden, a local group of garden volunteers. This will be followed by the opening of the plant sale where we will offer plants from local nurseries and growers. We are working to enable purchasers to obtain phytosanitary certificates for sending the plants outside of Canada.

One of the rock gardens on the Dalhousie Univeristy Agricultural Campus

Top left: Gerald Gloade   Top right: Alain Belliveau
Bottom left: The Wrightman family   Bottom right: Jiří Papoušek

The conference will feature both local speakers from Atlantic Canada and international speakers. On Thursday evening June 8, Gerald Gloade, naturalist and educator for the Mi'kmawey Debert Cultural Centre, will provide an "Introduction to Mi'kma'ki" explaining the development of the landscape of Nova Scotia since the last Ice Age through the legends of the Mi'kmaw people. This will be followed by Alain Belliveau, plant curator for the Irving Botanical Garden at Acadia University, who will speak on the "Wild Flowers of Nova Scotia."

On Friday evening, June 9, Esther Wrightman, operator of Wrightman's Rock Garden Nursery in St. Andrew's, New Brunswick, will speak on recent trends in rock garden plant cultivation and propagation. Julia Corden, from the UK, will also provide a talk on "Alpine Plants from Around the World." On the last evening of the conference, Saturday June 10, Jiří Papoušek from the Czech Republic will speak on his extensive rock gardening experience.

The talks will be in the evening to allow for bus tours during the day of our varied plant habitats and gardens in Nova Scotia. On Friday, one bus tour will visit a gypsum landscape to view rare plants and orchids as well as the Irving Arboretum at Acadia University that focuses on native plants and ecosystems. On Saturday, one tour will go to the coastal barrens near Peggy's Cove to see the seaside and bog plants as well as view a garden created on the barrens. Each day, we will have alternative tours of the Truro area for those who do not want such a long bus rides, almost two hours each way.

Peggy's Cove, Nova Scotia, Canada

Left: *Cypripedium acaule*   Right: *Arethusa bulbosa*

During the evenings, there will be the presentation of the various NARGS awards. The conference ends on Sunday, June 11, with optional tours of gardens in the area.

Travel to Nova Scotia

By Air

Halifax Airport is served by direct flights from a number of Canadian cities (Toronto, Montreal, Ottawa, Calgary and Vancouver), US cities (Boston, Philadelphia, and Newark), and Europe (London, Paris, Frankfurt). Connecting flights are available from anywhere in North America or Europe. The Dalhousie Agricultural Campus is 65 km (40 miles) from the Halifax Airport and can be reached through local bus service (twice daily at 12:45 and 3:50 pm, $14.25 Canadian) or limousine/shuttle service (cost approximately $140 Canadian for up to four passengers).

By Car (and sea)

Truro is about 9 ½ hours from Boston, 11 hours from Montreal or 13 hours from New York City driving on the highway. If you want an adventure along the way, you can take the Bar Harbor, Maine, to Yarmouth, Nova Scotia, catamaran ferry.

Accommodations

You have two choices for accommodation, staying on campus at the Dalhousie AC Residences, or staying at the Inn on Prince, about one mile from campus. The residence rooms are $38.50 single or $52.00 double a night, and the cost for the Inn on Prince is $129 per night, single or double. Full details available on our website: nargs23.org.

Registration

The conference registration, which includes speakers, tours, and meals from Thursday evening to Sunday morning (3 breakfasts, 2 lunches and 3 dinners) is set for $600 in Canadian dollars. With the current exchange rate this is less than the $450 US. Registration will open in early February 2023 and must be completed by May 18, three weeks before the start of the conference on June 8, 2023. We will post the link for the registration in early February on the conference website: NARGS23.org.

Waterfall at the Irving Arboretum at Acadia University

Post-Conference Tour
June 12-16 2023

This tour will leave Truro on Monday morning and travel to the Annapolis Valley with stops to see a population of *Cypripedium reginae*, if in flower, a private garden, or the rhododendrons at the Kentville Research Station with a stop to see Sand Barrens and the plant community there. Day one ends in Annapolis Royal.

Day Two (Tuesday) will include a tour of the Annapolis Royal Historic Gardens followed by a trip onto Long Island where we will follow a boardwalk to see skunk cabbage and other woodland plants on the way to see the Balancing Rock. From there, we will head for another ferry and cross over to Brier Island.

Day Three (Wednesday) will be spent on Brier Island exploring the various habitats including the Big Meadow Bog Restoration, the shore lines, and associated plants and the rare *Geum peckii* only known to be found on Long and Brier Islands and in the White Mountains in New Hampshire.

Day Four (Thursday) the tour leaves Brier Island and continues across country stopping at Bear River, the Tidal Village on Stilts, and passes through a wilderness area that includes Kejimkujik National Park and on to Liverpool where we will visit a woodland garden full of interesting plants and fantasy sculptures built by Ivan Higgins.

Day Five (Friday) opens up several choices on the way back to Halifax. A stop in Lunenburg, a UNESCO World Heritage Site, can be included, as well as revisiting the coastal barrens outside of Halifax and a visit to a couple of private gardens.

Termination of this tour will be late Friday afternoon either in Halifax, the Halifax International Airport, or Truro.

Opposite: Highlights of the post-conference tour.
Top left *Cypripedium reginae*   Top right: Balancing Rock
Bottom left: *Sarracenia* flowers   Bottom right: Sculptures by Ivan Higgins

President's Message

This issue will be going to press around the U.S.A.'s Thanksgiving, and I'm imagining all the Norman Rockwell-esque dinner tables where extended families are carefully avoiding talking about politics and religion. Except (of course) for that boorish uncle we all have who inevitably brings up one (or more) of the subjects! If you have the fortitude to read through to the bottom of this message, you might be grateful for some insights from this avuncular fellow who you just re-elected to serve another year to NARGS presidency!

Yesterday I attended a conference titled "Colorado Landscape Summit - Transformative Change for a Resilient Future" which consisted almost entirely of Water Utility managers from all over the entire state discussing how they would go about finding ways to drastically reduce, if not eliminate, lawns in their jurisdictions in the coming few years. Aurora (the second biggest city in Colorado) just did just this a few months ago for all new construction. The very first speaker at the Summit said "I'm not here suggesting we take out our bluegrass and put in rock gardens!" I'm pretty sure that speaker was not aware that NARGS existed, nor that its president was sitting a few dozen feet in front of him smiling wanly.

We rock gardeners generally regard what we do as a delightful pastime that gives us no end of aesthetic pleasure and wonderful insights into nature's exquisite artistry. We generally don't expect we'd annoy anyone beyond our spouse at times ("MUST you keep buying plants?") or perhaps a neighbor who looks askance at your miniature meadow just behind their Italianate fountain feature. I don't think many of us imagined that Utility managers are trembling at the thought of us banging on their doors with rocks and trowels. Surely none of us were planning to roll up and compost the bluegrass turf across all of North America (an area the size of Iowa I've read) and replace it with crevice gardens (although, come to think of it, I'm not entirely averse to the concept!).

Then I asked myself why would water Utility managers have even brought up the subject of rock gardens in that context? In a positive light, it means that the idea of rock gardening is out there. Lurking in the wings. Wafting on the ether, as it were. That gentleman didn't like the idea of rock gardens replacing bluegrass, but who knows? Maybe the next fellow who stands up will.

It's not out of the realm of possibility that I could be that very fellow. I've keynoted quite a few conferences in my day, why not this one? So I shall be prepared at the very next opportunity to say a few words on the subject. I need to practice. Read along and let me know what you think:

"Dear Water Utility providers! Thank you inviting me to address the potentially highly sensitive subject of bluegrass lawn replacement and our regional landscapes. Some have said we must not replace our vast expanses of bluegrass with rock gardens. I say, why not? Not necessarily intimate crevice gardens everywhere, but rock gardening is more than just rocks and alpines. Rock gardening is really about working with Nature. It encompasses a vast scope of gardening including woodlands, meadows, all manner of ground covers, perennials, bogs, and ponds. Heck, many of us grow cacti and desert plants, too. You could do far worse than enlist the membership of NARGS to help in this projected transformation.

"For one thing, what is needed to properly transform a virtually sterile monoculture like most lawns into a resilient, viable landscape is plant knowledge, which NARGS members possess in buckets. No one understands the subtleties of soil acidity/alkalinity, textures, the complexities of microclimate like a rock gardener. Most of us can grow extremely challenging plants from seed to bloom. In a perfect world, I would require your highway engineers and road maintenance crews to work with rock gardeners to make sure they chose the right plants and maintained them properly.

"Of course, the greatest obstacle to your mission of transforming landscapes is the complacence of the vast majority of non-rock gardening people (I call them "muggles") who are content with a threadbare lawn or a few half dead conifers in their "landscapes" and those who are addicted to "clean and green." I think you will find some push-back from muggles down the way if you remove vast stretches of bluegrass turf and replace it with river rock gravel or (shudder the thought) astroturf. Here, you could definitely enlist the help of rock gardeners who could show that a variety of plants woven together like a tapestry is far more attractive through the year than a flat expanse of just one taxon. And let's not even talk about the environmental benefits to pollinators, reducing the toxic application of herbicides and fertilizer runoff.

"I have informed the membership of my organization of your noble intentions to roll back the inexorable carpet of bluegrass that's consuming our pastures and prairies: I am quite sure they will rise, trowel in one hand, crow bar in the other, ready to take on the challenge!"

Unfortunately, I don't believe I shall have an opportunity to deliver this address where it ought to be given, but hope you might consider that the skills you learn in practicing rock gardening might indeed have far wider utility in the near future.

---Panayoti Kelaidis

North American Rock Garden Society
Year-End Report
December 2022

Dear NARGS Member,

We saw during 2022 the publication of *The Crevice Garden*, a landmark publication partially funded by NARGS, written by two of our dynamic young members. I think it's fair to say the book heralds a renaissance of our art as I have seen crevice gardens popping up at public gardens from coast to coast and also gracing more and more members' gardens. Let's not forget that rock gardens are not just plants and rocks. I believe our art is the epitome of sustainability—that overused but underutilized concept. For one thing they have sustained us, as all gardens did, during the worst of COVID in 2020 and 2021. Rock gardens, moreover, are laboratories mimicking natural ecosystems. Few rock gardeners utilize the arsenal of pesticides and chemicals that fill whole aisles of box stores. In the course of my half century of involvement in rock gardening, I have learned more from my fellow NARGS members than any other group about native plants, pollinators, and all facets of gardening. I am humbled and proud of our recent track record and promise.

A Look Back to 2022 and Look Forward to 2023

The year 2022 has so far been a good financial year for NARGS. It was the year we transitioned from a COVID-19 lockdown to a June Annual meeting in person in the Adirondacks, NARGS-sponsored tours, and traveling speakers for our local chapters. Local chapter meetings transitioned from all virtual to a mix of in-person and virtual meetings. Virtual study days continued to be extremely successful.

A large donation from an anonymous NARGS member early in 2022, a generous donation from the North American Heather Society as it discontinues operations, multiple virtual study days throughout the year, and the three in-person tours added significantly to NARGS income. *The Plants of Armenia* and *The Crevice Garden* book sales were a new source of income for

NARGS in 2022. The Traveling Speakers Tours were restarted in 2022 and are planned for expansion in 2023. NARGS ran a photo contest on Instagram and Facebook, managed by Mariel Tribby (Missouri). *The Rock Garden Quarterly* printing and shipping costs and the expense of our website conversion to Drupal 9 pushed expenses above our expectations. Despite all of the successes, we will continue to be dependent on membership renewals and year-end donations to cover our operating expenses for the remainder of 2022 and to get 2023 started off positively.

Seed Exchange

In the 2021-2022 Seed Exchange, we sent orders to 606 members in the Main Distribution, and filled another 244 orders in the Surplus Round. Currently, the Seed Exchange is working toward fulfilling requests from the 2022-2023 Seed List, which began on December 15. The thousands of seeds from hundreds of donors worldwide were divided and repackaged by 17 NARGS chapters and additionally by separate individuals. Orders in the Main Distribution will be filled through January by the Delaware Valley Chapter, and the Surplus Round of orders will be handled in March by the Great Lakes Chapter. All of the preparation and work has once again been organized by the Seed Intake Manager, Laura Serowicz (Michigan) with assistance from Joyce Fingerut (Connecticut). We greatly appreciate the timely, reliable, and capable help of all members who make our Seed Exchange internationally outstanding. This benefit remains an important means of attracting new members and maintaining the interest of current and longtime supporters.

NARGS Tours

Three tours in 2022, organized by David White (North Carolina), included a three-day tour of the Adirondacks in upstate New York; a twelve-day tour of the Bernese Oberland region of the Swiss Alps; and a seventeen-day tour of the Argentine Patagonia. NARGS is planning three foreign botanical tours in 2023 and 2024: a second tour to Argentine Patagonia (tentative dates are November 27 – December 13, 2023); a tour of the Lycian region of southwest Turkey focusing on early spring bulbs (tentative dates are February 26 – March 5, 2024); and a tour of Scandinavian gardens (late spring or early summer 2024). Registration for each of these tours will open approximately ten months prior to the tour dates.

NARGS Rocks Virtual Conferences

Our virtual conferences were very successful this year. "Succulents on the Rocks" was well received in January 2022, with over 270 tickets sold. We thank my co-host and speaker Rod Haenni (from Colorado and president of the Cactus & Succulent Society of America) for help with the project. Our February presentation, "Meadows," with Kenton Seth (Colorado) as co-host, was received with similar enthusiasm; there was the same number of viewers, but it attracted new members and current members from a different segment of our membership. A new tab "Videos" was added to our website menu under "Learn" where one might still purchase tickets to view the videos from these stellar virtual conferences should you have missed them or want to rewatch them. Our first FREE Video is also available to the public on the "Learn | Video" page. The video, a lecture report on the 2022 Norman Singer Grant recipients titled "Installing a Crevice Garden in Portland, Oregon" gives a detailed account of what it takes to build a crevice garden. Certainly, the masters, Jeremy Schmidt (North Carolina), Paul Spriggs (British Columbia), and Kenton Seth, make it all look so easy. Videos from the annual meeting lectures in Durango and Ithaca are free to all members and accessible from the menu item "Learn | Videos | Members Only Videos."

Website

The website, managed by Elisabeth Zander (Connecticut), has undergone a major software platform upgrade, now about 95% completed. A great new feature for winter armchair gardening is our "Learn | Sources" page. Depending on the category, it lists nurseries where plants are available for sale. Also, the list of allied plant societies will be found under that tab. One significant new change is NARGS' photos coming up on first page results in Google Searches. For example, when you do a Google search for *"Acantholimon saxifragiforme"* the results page shows the photo from nargs.org first, at the top of the result list. And those who use our Seed Exchange will notice direct access to NARGS' bank of plant photographs from the drill down feature of the Seedex listing.

Should you have a question about Traveling Speakers, the NARGS Bookstore, the Seed Exchange, membership, or issues with the website check out our members only email list of managers by going (while logged in) to "About Us | Boards & Staff | Members Only Email Contact" page. There you will find the email addresses for all administrators. And for those of you who have issues logging into the website, please be patient. We are still working on those routines. But remember you may always reach us by going to the top "Contact Us" button.

Traveling Speakers Program

The Traveling Speakers Program has emerged from pandemic-induced dormancy, and speakers who visited several chapters in 2022 included Kenton Seth and Paul Spriggs, Tom Freeth (United Kingdom), Kaj Andersen (Denmark), and Harry Jans (Netherlands). Plans are still being developed for 2023, and they include speaking tours by Todd Boland (Newfoundland) and Ian and Carole Bainbridge (United Kingdom). The program is funded by an anonymous, generous donor and headed by Rosemary Monahan (Massachusetts) who works in collaboration with six regional coordinators. Our website and the *Quarterly* will contain details of the 2023 program. Or, check with your local chapter leadership for speakers in your area.

Rock Garden Quarterly

As you saw in the January (winter) 2022 issue, Matt Mattus (Massachusetts) and our editor, Joseph Tychonievich (Indiana), have finished a redesign of the look of the *Quarterly's* cover and pages, and there are new projects in the works. Joseph is always on the lookout for talented rock gardeners, who might also write an article for the *Quarterly*. Unfortunately, many potential writers simply don't have the time. So, in the upcoming winter issue, as in the fall issue, you'll see interviews as a way to get the insights and experience of these talented gardeners. I'm excited how these have turned out, and I hope these interviews will keep bringing new perspectives to future issues.

Your Continued Financial Support is Appreciated

Your continuing individual membership helps support the Seed Exchange, annual meetings and study weekends, and our publication, *The Rock Garden Quarterly*. However, membership dues only partially cover these activities that you value. Your annual donation to NARGS is needed to make up the difference. We hope you will make a donation online on the NARGS Web site at www.nargs.org. Click on the "Donate" button on the upper part of the home page. Or you may donate when you renew your membership. You may donate online using your credit card or your PayPal account. Or you may donate by check in U.S. funds (payable to NARGS) or by mailing credit card information to: NARGS, POB 18604, Raleigh, NC 27619-8604 USA. In the U.S., NARGS is a 501(c)(3) tax-exempt organization, and your donation may be tax deductible to the extent permitted by law.

Now as climate change looms ever more ominously, I believe our rock gardens will be prototypes and testing grounds for more viable groundcovers and garden plants for a viable future. Our society has held well-attended Annual General Meetings when most other groups cancelled theirs—and we are expanding our vision in conservation and relevance each passing year. Now more than ever NARGS has risen to the occasion!

Thank you for helping NARGS remain a champion of the North American gardening community.

Respectfully,

Panayoti Kelaidis

Panayoti Kelaidis (President) on behalf of NARGS Officers, Board of Directors, and NARGS Support Team

Nominations for Online Election
May 1 through May 14, 2023

Recommended by the NARGS Nominating Committee, consisting of Ed Glover, chair; Mike Bone, Brendan Kenney, Terry Laskiewicz, Tony Reznicek, Sarah Strickler, and Bobby Ward.

Panayoti Kelaidis nominated for president (Colorado): "My love of rock gardening goes back to my childhood in the 1950s, growing up in Boulder under the shadow of the Rockies, inspired by Paul Maslin's masterpiece rock garden a few blocks away, and helping my brother-in-law build my first garden at my parent's house when I was barely 10 years old. Fast forward more than a half century--I have not only helped create the Rock Alpine Garden at Denver Botanic Gardens, but have spoken at most NARGS chapters repeatedly, and visited dozens of rock gardens around the globe expanding my understanding of the art. My vision for NARGS is for us to pave the way for the Millennial generation to come aboard as members and eventually take the helm and move our society onto a much wider scope and really pave the way for rock gardens and rock plants in every home and garden." [Panayoti is currently serving as president and is eligible for another one-year term.]

Todd Boland nominated for vice president (Newfoundland): Todd lives in St. John's, Newfoundland, where he works as the chief horticulturist at the Memorial University of Newfoundland Botanical Garden. He is the chairperson of the Newfoundland chapter of NARGS. Since 2009, he has been the author of the NARGS website "Plant of the Month" feature and is the administrator of the on-line image gallery. He is a regular contributor to *The Rock Garden Quarterly* and has spoken to gardening groups across North America as well as in the U.K. and New Zealand. He has published six botanical guides to the flora of Atlantic Canada and most recently published his first gardening book *Perennials*

for Atlantic Canada. His companion guide, *Shrubs and Vines for Atlantic Canada* was released spring 2021. [Todd is currently serving as vice-president and is eligible for another one-year term.]

Sarah Strickler nominated for recording secretary (Virginia): "A NARGS and Potomac Valley Chapter member since 2009, I have served as program chair and newsletter editor for our chapter. I spent more than 30 years in book publishing, my last position as marketing manager for a niche publisher. Once bitten by the horticulture bug, I was also employed as a gardener at the U.S. National Arboretum for six years, where I rotated throughout the collections. I recently closed my small garden maintenance and design business and returned to the Arboretum in a term position, working on programs in the education unit. Keeping rock plants alive in my Arlington, Virginia, garden can be challenging due to increasingly hot, wet, and humid summers, but I try anyway. Trips with NARGS to the Italian Dolomites and Scotland were a big inspiration as I'm sure the upcoming Patagonia excursion will be. I welcome the chance to help NARGS move forward." [Sarah is currently serving as recording secretary and is eligible for another two-year term.]

Richard Lane nominated for treasurer (North Carolina): Richard H. Lane is owner of Lane Financial Services in Raleigh, North Carolina, where he specializes in internal audit and individual income tax consulting. Previously, he was the General Auditor for First Citizens Bank, an Audit Director for the Bank of America (formerly NCNB), and General Auditor for the Bank of North Carolina. He has been a part of audit management at the manager, director, and chief audit executive level for 25 years. He is a Certified Internal Auditor, a Certified Financial Services Auditor, a Certified Public Accountant, a Chartered Bank Auditor, and a Certified Information Systems Auditor. [Richard is currently serving as treasurer and is eligible for another two-year term.]

Carol Eichler for Director of the Board (New York):

"As a 20+ year member of the Adirondack Chapter and of NARGS, I have been an advocate for rock gardening. I have taught public rock gardening classes and continue to lead the on-going volunteer effort to maintain our chapter's 22-year old public rock garden. To keep our chapter strong I have served in just about every leadership role including Chair, Program Chair, Newsletter Editor, Seed Exchange Coordinator, and Secretary/Treasurer. At the national level I served as Chair of the highly successful (by all counts) 2022 AGM in Ithaca and the cancelled 2020 AGM. For these combined efforts I was honored to receive NARGS' Marvin Black Award. As a NARGS Board member I look forward to offering my strong organizational skills and my professional background in marketing and fundraising to further NARGS' goals as a strong and vibrant organization for generations to come." [Carol would be elected for a three-year term to the Board.]

Patrick Ion for Director of the Board (Michigan):

Patrick Ion was president of the Great Lakes Chapter of NARGS from 2013 until 2016 and had the honor of being host president for the national meeting in Ann Arbor. He retired in 2011 after 30 years as an editor of the world's database of mathematical research, Mathematical Reviews and MathSciNet, located at the University of Michigan. His career had taken him to posts in the U.K., U.S., Holland, Japan, Germany, France, and New Zealand. Patrick also chaired a W3C standards working group, an open web platform for application development. He has had a garden with his wife, Bonnie, in Ann Arbor, Michigan, for the past 37 years, and he is serving as Great Lake Chapter's webmaster. [Patrick would be elected for a three-year term to the Board.]

 **Janice Currie** for Director of the Board (British Columbia): "I rock garden in the Pacific Northwest in Victoria, British Columbia. We have mountains and ocean for inspiration and a plethora of stratified stone to choose from when building homes for rock and alpine plants. I am a huge advocate of nature-inspired troughs and crevice gardens, particularly built with tufa sourced here in British Columbia. I grow alpines from seed and cuttings shared from sources close to home and of course the NARGS seed exchange. I am the president of the Vancouver Island Rock and Alpine Garden Society in Victoria. Our club has been home to many well-known rock gardeners over the years. I'd be honoured to lend a hand in strengthening ties with Pacific Northwest members and groups." [Janice would be elected for a three-year term to the Board.]

From-the-Floor Nominations

Election of President, Vice President, Recording Secretary, Treasurer, and three Board Members

The names of those proposed by the Nominating Committee can be viewed on the NARGS website <www.nargs.org> and in this issue of the *Quarterly*. There is now opportunity for members to nominate FROM THE FLOOR no later than January 31, 2023.The combined list of candidates will be published on the NARGS website by April 1 and in the spring 2023 Quarterly (dispatched no later than the end of March 2023).

Online election will be held May 1 through May 14, 2023. All active members will be mailed a link shortly before the election opens. Your email address will admit you. If you are a member and have never verified your email address, please do so as soon as possible. You may contact Bobby Ward for help. The www.nargs.org website will have a notice when voting begins, as well as a copy of the voting-site link on the News page.

A from-the-floor nomination for any post may be emailed to Ed Glover, Nominating Committee Chair no later than January 31, 2023.

The Nomination must include: name, chapter (if applicable), email address, a position for which each person is nominated. The nominee must be a member of NARGS. Bio of the nominee (100 words or less, written by nominee) Picture of nominee (shoulder length) Note of acceptance from nominee indicating a willingness to serve if elected.

All nominations and required nominee information must be received by January 31, 2023.

[To contact Ed or Bobby, log on to the NARGS Web site and click on "About Us" and then click on "Members Only Contact Page."]

NARGS Donations

Donations to NARGS between August 1 and October 31, 2022,
Designated for the General Fund.

Anderson, Scott, St. Louis, MO
Clark, Susan, Concord, MA
Krohn, Karen, Quaker Hill, CT
Ulmann, Mary Ann and Chuck, West Chester, PA
Ward, Bobby J., Raleigh, NC

The following recently became NARGS Patrons:

Adelman, Elizabeth (Wisconsin)
Bell, Lynne (Oregon)
Brown, Alison (Maine)
Caicco, Steve (Washington)
Caroff, Julia (Michigan)
Davies, Robert (New York)
DeRouin, Cecile (Florida)
Drzyzgula, Cathy (Oregon)
Fitzpatrick, John (Maryland)
Hughes, James (Maryland)
Jaynes, Craig (Ohio)
Lofgren, Aaron (Minnesota)
Parish, Ivy (California)
Pulman, David (Georgia)
Redmond, Janalee (Maryland)
Rousseau, Margaret (Maine)
Willis, John (Maryland)

New and Rejoining Members

Welcome to all those who joined or rejoined between
August 1 and November 14, 2022

Almanzor, Janine, Riverdale, CA

Bekken, Gunnar, Storen, Norway

Bell, Lynne, Corbett, OR

Belsky, Xanthe E., Campo, CA

Bertoncini, David, Mishawaka, IN

Briese, Katharina, Bad Pyrmont, Germany

Callinan, Veronica, Toronto, ON

Cameron, Dugald, Toronto, ON

Carter, Bill, Winona, MN

Clark, Logan, Cary, NC

Clegg, John, Chicago, IL

Collins, Kathleen, Oakland, CA

Courtens, Jean-Paul & Crystal, Johnstown, NY

Davies, Robert, New York, NY

Dowd, Leanne Kiss, Neepawa, MB

Dreiffus, Donald, Claremont, NH

Elkins, Judith, Prineville, OR

Ensign, Lila E., Fort Worth, TX

Ford, Patricia, Durango, CO

Freeth, Tom, West Molesy, United Kingdom

Fritsch, Brittany, Denver, CO

Fruge, Romaine, Hyde Park, NY

Galvez, Kathleen, Staten Island, NY

Genender, Nazarena, Durango, CO

Graham, John, Wantage, United Kingdom

Hansen, Richard, Livermore, CA

Hardy, Kevin, Grand Junction, CO

Havelka, Theresa, Sacramento, CA

Hiemstra, Idske, Evergreen, CO

Hopper, Roxane, Pecos, NM

Horn, Dora, Santa Fe, NM

Hunt, Colin, Hazelbrook, NSW, Australia

Jenkins, Edwin, Sevierville, TN

Johnson, Shane, Victoria, BC

Kelly, Leslie, Centennial, CO

Khalil, Alexandria, Jenkintown, PA

Krofft, Claire, Webster Groves, MO

Kurihara, Anna, North Hollywood, CA

Lee, Maggie, Santa Fe, NM

Lisk, Susan, San Antonio, TX

Mackay, Ewan, Toronto, ON

Massey, Mary, Verona, WI

McCloud, Cheryl, Mokelumne Hill, CA

Meny, Joe, Washington, DC

Mertz, Susan, Powell Gardens, Kingsville, MO

Miller, Sandra, Denver, CO

Milliken, James, Bellevue, WA

Morash, Justin, Darmouth, NS

Mráz, Jan, Planá nad Luznicí, Czech Republic

Nattier, Mark, Tarrytown, NY

Normand, Lisa, Calgary, AB

Nygard, Rowan, Kennett Square, PA

Oliver, Christina, Bellingham, WA

Peace, Tom, Denver, CO

Poteet, David, Canandaigua, NY

Princz, Marina, Vancouver, BC

Ross, Jacqueline, Berwyn, IL

Rubenstein, Patricia, Edina, MN

Schenot, Kate, Seattle, WA

Sheffield, Stephanie, Lexington, KY

Stageman, Donald, Holland, MI

Steenhoudt, Karen, Radnor, PA

Stodder, Lisa, Michigan City, IN

Thomas, Lindsey, Evergreen, CO

Tindall, Kathy, Seattle, WA

Wyndham, Susan, Newark, DE

Seed Exchange

We really appreciate the time and effort spent by the NARGS members, including many new donors, who have donated seeds to our Seed Exchange this year. It has been a fraught gardening season in many ways in many places, but we are grateful that many of you have contributed despite the extraordinary challenges.

Once again the Delaware Valley (Main Distribution) and Great Lakes (Surplus Round) chapters are responding to your seed requests. Orders in the Main Distribution will be accepted by Delaware Valley until January 31. The Great Lakes volunteers will begin filling Surplus Round orders on March 1, with a deadline of March 17 to receive your requests.

Our chapters can continue to feed their need for seed by opting in when we offer them a final distribution of the remaining items – which often include many interesting and useful taxa. Chapter Chairs should promptly respond to my notice early March to indicate whether they would like a portion of these seeds, free of charge.

We regret that members in Japan, the UK, the EU, and Australia may place orders only in the Main Distribution. Their countries require phytosanitary certificates for all imported seeds and, due to the costs and work involved, we cannot provide that service twice each year. We request that members are careful to order only those seeds that are allowed to be imported into their countries; otherwise the entire shipment to their country's Consignee might be refused by customs officers: One ineligible packet can jeopardized everyone's orders.

I also remind our stateside members that many states have their own lists of plants that are prohibited. While officials are unlikely to check the mails and confiscate seeds, we should all be aware of taxa that could be problematic in our local ecosystems.

If you intend to place a seed order from our website, please be certain that Executive Secretary Bobby Ward has the most up-to-date email address for you, so that the electronic ordering system can recognize you as a current member in good standing.

If you want to place an order using the print copy of the Seed List and order form, contact me immediately:

Joyce Fingerut
537 Taugwonk Road
Stonington, CT 06378-1805
U.S.A.
1-860-535-3067

Nota Bene: Due to website security issues, in order to reach us via the NARGS website, you now need to log in, check the "About Us" column, and go to the "Members Only Email Contact Page" to find our names and email addresses. Or use the "Contact Us" link in the top menu and select "Seed Exchange" from the Category box to direct an email to us. This roundabout method is the only way to keep our website safe for everyone to use.

I hope that you all receive the seeds you most desire, and that they germinate and fulfill your expectations.

Joyce Fingerut

Director, NARGS Seed Exchange

[To contact Joyce or Bobby, log on to the NARGS Web site and click on "About Us" and then click on "Members Only Email Contact Page."]

NARGS Traveling Speakers Program

Plans are actively being developed to bring exciting speakers to chapters across North America in 2023, so please check the NARGS website for updates. Speaking engagements so far include:

Midwest Region and Canadian Region

Ian and Carole Bainbridge, Scottish Rock Garden Club and other affiliations

• Late March and early April. Chapters, dates and topics to be decided.

Southeast/Mid-Atlantic Region:

Todd Boland, Research Horticulturist at Memorial University of Newfoundland

• March 18, Raleigh, NC. Piedmont Chapter. Spring Alpines of the Spanish Aragonian Pyrenees

• Date and topic to be decided. Potomac Valley Chapter

• Date and topic to be decided. Four Seasons Garden Club

• March 25. Delaware Valley Chapter. Spring Wildflowers of Utah's Mighty Five Great Parks

• March 26. Allegheny Chapter. Topic to be decided.

Check the NARGS website or your chapter chair for updates and any changes to schedules.

--Rosemary Monahan

To contact Rosemary, click the "Contact Us," next to the "Log in" button and type "Speakers Tour" in the subject line.

Upcoming NARGS Webinars

January 14, 2023: Small Woodies

(Ericaceous plants, conifers, and more).

Co-hosts: Todd Boland with Jamie Ellison, Tony Reznicek, and Sandy Horn

February 25, 2023: What's New in Rock Gardening (Building a moveable mountain, propagation techniques, and more).

Co-host: Paul Spriggs with Razvan Chisu, Esther Benedict, and Chris Dixon

Check the NARGS website for details and how to register.

Meeting Stipend

The NARGS board has approved up to five meeting stipends per year for five NARGS chapter members who have never attended a national NARGS meeting (excluding one that the local chapter hosted). The stipend will cover the registration cost of the meeting. Local chapters are encouraged to match the amount to help further defray the cost of the member attending the meeting. The application requires approval of the local chair who forwards to the NARGS president for approval. If the NARGS member does not belong to a local chapter, the request will go directly to the NARGS president.

The application form is located on the NARGS web site under "About Us" and then go to "Members News" and click on "Meeting Stipend." You will need to log in to access the site.

NARGS Book Service

The NARGS Book Service has received a fresh influx of books from a member's storage shed. These are books that were rescued when the original Book Store was discontinued. So, these are new oldies but goodies.

The Caucasus and its Flowers by Holubec and Krivka. A coffee table book. Pictures with descriptions of plants. Hardcover, 390 pages. Originally 96 Euros, now $30. 10 copies.

Handbook on Troughs by NARGS. Paperback 76 pages. $7 each, or 10 for $35 for NARGS Chapters. 139 copies.

Lychnis and Silene in the Garden by James L Jones and NARGS. Paperback, 84 pages. Pictures and descriptions. $5. 15 copies.

A History of the American Rock Garden Society by Marnie Flook. Paperback, 206 pages. The history of what is now NARGS from 1934 to 1995. $5. 5 copies.

Utah Wildflowers – A Field Guide to Northern and Central Mountains and Valleys by Richard Shaw/Utah State University Press. Paperback, 218 pages, plants arranged by colors. Describes plants and growing conditions and characteristics. $10. 6 copies.

Northwest Penstemons by Dee Strickler. Hardcover, 191 pages. 80 Species native to the Pacific Northwest. Detailed descriptions/drawings/pictures/maps. $15. 6 copies.

Bulbs of North America by NARGS. Hardcover, 251 pages plus 50 pages of pictures. 8 groupings of plants and 3 geographical groupings. $17. 7 copies.

Rock Garden Design and Construction by NARGS. Hardback 316 pages. A collection of monographs by various authors. Principles/materials/types/structure/ regional styles. $15. 73 copies.

Prices include postage (which is being paid by a NARGS donor). Sorry, but mail-order sales in the U.S. only.

Questions? Contact Book Service Volunteer, Dave Collura. To reach Dave, click the "Contact Us," next to the "Log in" button. And put "Book Service" in the subject line.

NARGS Tours & Adventures in 2023 and 2024

NARGS is planning three foreign botanical tours in 2023 and 2024: a second tour to Argentine Patagonia that will be similar to the 2022 Patagonia tour; a tour of the Lycian region of southwest Turkey that will focus on early spring bulbs; and a tour of Scandinavian gardens. Tentative dates are November 27 – December 13, 2023, for the Patagonia tour and February 26 – March 5, 2024 for the Lycia, Turkey, tour. The schedule for the Scandinavia tour has not been set but is expected to be in late spring or early summer of 2024.

Registration for each of these tours will open approximately ten months prior to the tour dates. Details for each of the tours will be announced via email and will be posted on the NARGS website.

--David White, chair

[To contact David, log on to the NARGS Web site and click on "About Us" and then click on "Members Only Email Contact Page."]

Norman Singer Endowment Applications Due March 15, 2023

NARGS expects to award grants in 2023 to one or more projects that advance the art and science of rock gardening. Guidelines for submittal of applications and selection of projects, as well as the application form, are posted on line. The deadline for submittal of applications is March 15, 2023. Grant recipients will be announced in June at the NARGS annual meeting in Truro, Nova Scotia. For information on the grants and how to apply, log on to the web site and click on "About Us" and then "Grants."

NARGS Awards Nominations
Due March 15, 2023

Nominations are due to Cyndy Cromwell, chair of the Awards Committee, by March 15, 2023. Send electronic nominations only, please. To submit an entry, log on to the NARGS Web site and click on "About Us" and then click on "Members Only Email Contact Page."

Awards will be announced in June at the NARGS annual meeting in Truro, Nova Scotia.

Award of Merit: Established in 1965, this award is given to persons who have made outstanding contributions to rock and alpine gardening and to the North American Rock Garden Society. In addition, the recipients will be people of demonstrated plantsmanship. The recipient must be an active member of the Society.

Marcel Le Piniec Award: Established in 1969, this award is given to a nursery person, propagator, hybridizer, or plant explorer who is currently actively engaged in extending and enriching the plant material available to rock gardeners. This may be a joint award if two people have worked closely together. The recipient need not be a member of NARGS.

Edgar T. Wherry Award: Established in 1973, this award is given from time to time to a person who has made an outstanding contribution in the dissemination of botanical and/or horticultural information about native North American plants. The works must be scientifically sound, but may be written for popular readership and do not have to be specifically about rock garden plants. Generally, the award recognizes a body of work or a lifetime of literary effort rather than a single work (see the Carleton R. Worth Award). The recipient does not have to be a member of the Society.

Carleton R. Worth Award: Established in 1985, this award is given to an author of distinguished writings about rock gardening and rock garden plants in a book or in magazine articles. The Award may also be based on an Editor's body of work for a Chapter Newsletter. The recipient does not have to be a member of the Society.

Marvin E. Black Award: Established in 1990, this award is given to a member of the Society who excels at promoting membership in NARGS; organizing study weekends, national, and international meetings. They should also be involved in such activities as planning trips to study plants and to meet other plant people. The emphasis shall be placed on a member who has helped other people to reach their potential in the plant world. The recipient must be a member of the Society.

Linc & Timmy Foster Millstream Garden Award: Established in 2006, this award is for an outstanding contribution to the North American Rock Garden Society for creating a superior garden. This is not meant to be a competition, but to recognize members' great gardens across the various styles and regions of the United States and Canada. Since there is such a wide range of possibilities in style and climate regions, it has been decided there needs to be four categories of gardens. They are: the Container Garden, the Alpine Rock Garden, the Woodland Garden and the Special Garden. Any of these gardens must be a private garden to eliminate unfair institutional advantages. This award is meant to reward the creation of gardens, which meet a wide standard set by the North American Rock Garden Society, and reflects well on that society. The Millstream award should be submitted with a short one-page essay (300-500 words--that can be published in *The Rock Garden Quarterly*) with 3-7 images (preferably sent at 1 MB, but with higher resolution backup available if the garden is to be featured in the *Quarterly*). The recipient must be a member of the Society.

Frank Cabot Public Garden Award: Established in 2018 this award is given to a public garden that excels in furthering the purpose of the North American Rock Garden Society in promoting the construction and design of rock gardens; the cultivation, conservation, and knowledge of rock garden plants and their geographical distribution; and the public outreach through plant exploration and introduction of new garden-worthy species. The award is limited to great public gardens in the United States and Canada that meet high standards in the creation of public rock gardens. Since there is such a wide range of possibilities in climate and geographic regions, there are four categories of public gardens that may be considered for the award. They are: the Container Garden, the Alpine Rock Garden, the Woodland Garden, and the Special Garden. The Frank Cabot Public Garden Award should be submitted with a short one-page essay (300-500 words--that can be published in *The Rock Garden Quarterly*) with 3-7 images (preferably sent at 1 MB, but with higher resolution backup available if the garden is to be featured in the *Quarterly*).

[To contact Cyndy or submit an entry, log on to the NARGS Web site and click on "About Us" and then click on "Members Only Email Contact Page."]

--Cyndy Cromwell, chair

We have learned of the death of the following NARGS members:

Helen Herold, Carlisle, Massachusetts
Bobby G. Wilder, Raleigh, North Carolina

Rock, Alpine, and Allied Garden Societies

Alpine Garden Club of British Columbia: www.agc-bc.ca

Alpine Garden Society (U.K.): www.alpinegardensociety.net

American Conifer Society: www.conifersociety.org

American Penstemon Society: https://penstemons.org

American Primrose Society: www. americanprimrosesociety.org

American Rhododendron Society: www.rhododendron.org

British Cactus & Succulent Society: www.bcss.org.uk

Cactus & Succulent Society of America: www.cactusandsucculentsociety.org

Cyclamen Society: www.cyclamen.org

Dutch Rock Garden Society: www.nrvwebsite.nl

Dwarf Iris Society: www.dwarfiris.org

Eriogonum Society: www.eriogonum.org

Flemish Rock Garden Society: www.vrvforum.be

Fritillaria Group (U.K.): www.fritillaria.org.uk

New Zealand Alpine Garden Society: www.nzags.com

Pacific Bulb Society: www.pacificbulbsociety.org

Rock Gardeners Club Prague: https://skalnickari.cz/

Scottish Rock Garden Club: www.srgc.net

Species Iris Group of North America: http://www.signa.org/index.pl?Intro

Victoria Island Rock & Alpine Garden Society: www.virags.com

Of Additional Interest

Norman Deno's "Seed Germination Theory and Practice" (1993): https://naldc.nal.usda.gov/download/41278/PDF

International Rock Gardener: https://www.srgc.net/international_rock_gardener.asp

Ian Young's Bulb Log Diary: https://www.srgc.net/bulblog.asp

Hardy Plant Society (various groups in the U.S.)

NARGS Service Awards

Ewan Mackay (Ontario Chapter): Over the last 13 years, Ewan Mackay has been instrumental in guiding the society's website and electronic communications, including the electronic development of the Germination Guide and Seedex. In 2009 Ewan volunteered to help steer us towards a modern website. He supported the board in hiring a local developer for a Drupal based Content Management System (CMS) website and took the lead role working with the developer, and then went on to manage the website after it went live in 2011. After the developer stopped support, the website was too costly to update and maintain.

Ewan identified Sherill Allard as a possible way forward and supported her as she offered to develop a new website using Joomla CMS, an easier system to work with. Both Ewan and Sherill were able to take free online training needed to develop and maintain the new site which went live in 2020.

Ewan helped develop digital communication policies as he prepared and distributed the monthly journal via news@ onrockgarden.com to an ever-growing number of recipients, saving thousands of dollars on printing and mailing. He also prepares the Ontario's annual member seed exchange (Seedex) list. To support this in 2011 he created the electronic Master Germination Guide (GG), which is now found on our website where a visitor can find the germination requirements of any of over 9000 seeds previously listed in the Seedex. (Submitted by Sherill Allard and seconded by Arie Vanspronsen).

Veronica Callinan (Ontario Chapter): Since Veronica Callinan joined the Ontario Rock Garden & Hardy Plant Society in 2008, she has made many significant contributions of leadership and support for the group. From 2010 to 2015, Veronica held positions of Vice-Chair, Chair and past Chair. During this time, she served on the nominating committee, helped with our booth at public events and recruited volunteers for our plant sales.

Her advice has been invaluable as we began accepting credit card payments at our sales. In March 2014, she presented a Members Showcase entitled "Berge und Burgen." Our publication, The Journal, carried an article by Veronica, "Backyard Habitats." From 2014 to 2022, she has been an administrator of our Facebook page, recently introducing a feature requesting a new group picture each month. For the past year, she has assisted in hosting our activities on Zoom. Her other activities have been hosting garden tours (2010, 2017, and 2019) and regular participation in the annual Seedex.(Submitted by Carol Clark and seconded by Arie Vanspronsen)

Patrice Van Vleet and **Glenn Guenterberg** (Rocky Mountain Chapter): This dynamic duo have been leaders of the Rocky Mountain Chapter of NARGS since they first joined serving our club in many ways, not the least of which was serving as president! They are always there, ready to help—whether driving a busload of tour participants to Cody and the Bighorns, or staging club events, or hosting visitors. Their extraordinary garden near Roxborough is studded with extraordinary crevice gardens and boasts meadows of color, woodlands, and exquisite troughs. (Submitted by Sandy Snyder)

Greg Hewgley (Rocky Mountain Chapter): Greg joined the club in 2013 and was already serving as secretary by 2015, serving till 2018. He was very thorough with his notes and kept all of us on the board quite in line. He was a great support to me as a vice president after Rod Haenni in the 2nd DC ("During Covid") year of 2021. He found very interesting speakers, organized a great garden tour which included an entire lot just-for and just-planted as a rock garden by Lisa Negri. He continued innovations by implementing the use of bar codes with help of the Colorado Cactus and Succulent Society for our spring plant sale. (Submitted by Kathleen Stewart).

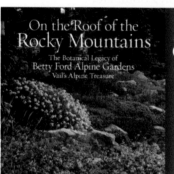

NARGS Chapters (meeting place/area) and Chairpersons or Co-Chairs

Adirondack (Ithaca, NY)	John Gilrein
Alaska (Anchorage & Mat-Su Valley)	Florene Carney
Allegheny (Pittsburgh, PA)	Nancy Knauss
Berkshire (Stockbridge, MA)	Vacant
Calgary Rock & Alpine Garden Society (Calgary, AB)	
	Patti O'Keefe
Columbia-Willamette (Portland, OR)	Jane McGary
Delaware Valley (Philadelphia, PA)	Louise Clarke
Fells (Newbury, NH)	Thelma Hewitt
Gateway (St. Louis, MO)	Mariel Tribby
Great Lakes (Southern MI)	Julia Caroff
Hudson Valley (Westchester Co, NY)	Don Dembowski
Long Island (Oyster Bay, NY)	Donald Ohl
Manhattan (New York, NY)	Judith Dumont
Minnesota (Minneapolis/St. Paul, MN)	Rick Rodich
New England (Waltham/Boylston, MA)	Estelle James
Newfoundland (St. John's, NL)	Todd Boland
New Mexico (Santa Fe/Albuquerque, NM)	Robin Magowan
Northwestern (Seattle, WA)	Kendall McLean
Nova Scotia (Halifax & Truro, NS)	Roslyn Duffus
Ohio Valley (OH & surrounding states)	Joan Day
Ontario (Don Mills, ON)	David Pounds
Ottawa Valley (Ottawa, ON)	Rob Stuart and Jane Lund
Piedmont (Raleigh, NC)	Cyndy Cromwell
Potomac Valley (Alexandria, VA)	Barbara Rose
Québec (Montreal, QC)	Pierre Morrissette
Rocky Mountain (Denver, CO)	Panayoti Kelaidis
Sierra (Sonora, CA)	Nancy Piekarczyk
Siskiyou (Medford, OR)	Jean Buck
Wasatch (Salt Lake City, UT)	Tony Stireman
Watnong (Far Hills, NJ)	Roxanne Hiltz
Western (San Francisco Bay area, CA)	(vacant)
Wisconsin-Illinois (Madison-Chicago)	Dave Collura

To obtain the email addresses for the chapter chairs, log on to NARGS and click
on "About Us" and then click on "Chapter Contact."
https://www.nargs.org/local-chapters